Gyroscape

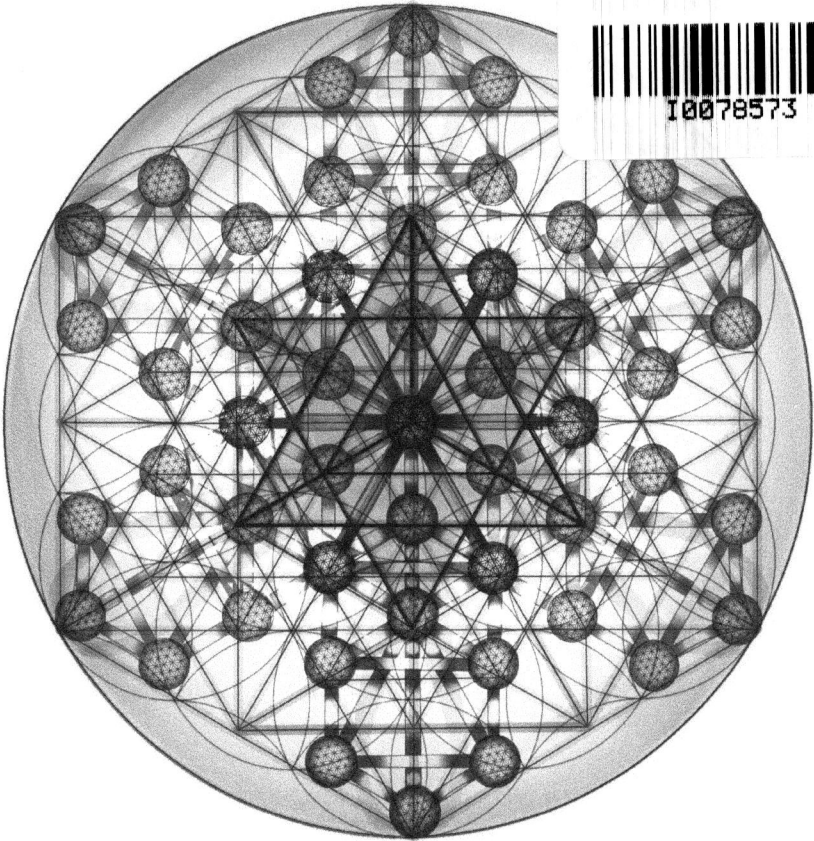

Spherical Spins In Lyrical Verse

Indi Riverflow

Gyroscape:
Spherical Spins in Lyrical Verse
Indi Riverflow

ISBN-13: 978-0692203590
ISBN-10: 0692203591

Design and images by
Amana Mission All-In-One Media Magician

Undying gratitude to John Kadlecik & JKB for making it happen.

*If you would like to adapt any lyric within this volume for musical composition or reprint, please contact us via e-mail at **ampi@amanamission.com***

More writing from Indi Riverflow abounds
*Please visit **www.amanamission.com** to stay current*

Amana Mission Publishing Ink
Alternative Press

To Incite Insight

www.amanamission.com

Table of Context

Surreal Cortex:
In It to Spin It

The human mind perceives patterns. Generally, it can be dangerous to generalize too broadly about the protean properties of mentality, but this particular faculty, detecting repetition, seems more or less intrinsic to the conscious condition. We are model-makers, replicating all of Nature in miniature.

Our world is a swirl of smoke and mirrors, estimations nested in layers of recursive reflection, assembling perspectives in flipping frames, evolving into sensations of relation. Some internal virtual wizard, cloaked behind curtains of continuity, whips up a custom-crafted carnival of whirling wonders, which appears to be a flawless facsimile of the fractal hologram humanity regards as home.

The resonance of these patterns, imported by whatever sense organ is capable of capturing them, form the synaptic latticework connecting the dots of diverse dimensions. Eyes detect, and minds define, intricate patterns of photons dancing on myriad surfaces, and we call this *sight*. Ears distinguish and combine patterns of audible wave frequencies in the vicinity, and we call this *sound*. Clocks organize events in sequence and we call this *time*.

The carnival is always open, and the mind is always being taken for a ride, one way or another. Dizzy and disoriented, we strut and stumble from carousel to roller-coaster, clutching our precious tickets. Crafty barkers lure the blurry masses into traps of petty hustles and cheap thrills, while wiser eyes depend on a wider variety of news and reviews to steer an independent course of festivity.

Hordes of tourists tour the horrors of haunted houses, marveling at oddities, spinning in recursive halls of mirrors. Some are busy trying their hands at contests of random chance or trivial skill, or applauding acrobatic demonstrations of freakish ability.

Always in pursuit of adventure, thrill-seekers hop blithely into secured seats which rise and plunge for the sake of vertigo, periodically pausing for routines of biology, ever tending to the all-important supply of tickets.

We tend to expend much of our lives in line, hurrying to wait, converting time into tickets and tickets into time, seeking entertaining ways to pass the days, while anxiously fretting over how little time remains. Gathering in restless throngs, we mill about, hunting desperately for better games to play, more talented acts to gawk at, and always worrying about the ticket stacks.

One way or another, most of us are on the clock most of the time. Unable to afford perpetual entertainment, the majority are laboring to procure their own tickets, often by way of menial, tedious, even extorted performances. On payday, rarely a breath is wasted before rushing off to redeem them in yet another long line, winding around the next fleeting diversion.

Some eventually sense that much of the carnival is pure sham, anything but fair, promising spectacles in tents which are ultimately empty: an engineered synthetic environment designed to capture your soul and empty your pockets.

Disillusioned, they wander out of the amusement park to seek superior distraction and meaning. Many never return, disdaining the din of jaded carnies and their unwitting marks for the rest of their days.

Others are driven, by some imperative of compassion, to return, in order to enhance the collective carnival and improve matters. Finding that the structure of the show is flawed, these visionaries endeavor to reinvent entertainment entirely. They become ringleaders of new circuses, and the cycle repeats.

Repeating cycles are woven into the very fabric of what we call existence, from particles to planets to galaxies, and presumably, beyond. This grand design is a pattern-quilt, cut from whole cloth and sewn together by threads of consciousness.

The nuts and bolts of reality may not truly be there at all; under the microscope, what we usually think of as "matter" might be better regarded as simply a specific magnitude of vibrations. Particles exhibit a wave nature, blurring the line between being and becoming.

Body, *mind*, and *spirit* are not distinct components of a living being, but rather different ways of considering the same entity: as *form*, as *awareness*, and as *essence*. Applying this principle across cosmic and microcosmic scales is where physics and metaphysics intersect.

It was once believed that the basic, irreducible unit of the Universe would turn out to be the atom, which has since been shown to consist of largely vast empty spaces bounded by electron clouds. Everywhere scientists turn their lenses, emptiness dwarfs form, and certainty vanishes.

When the scale penetrates to the sub-atomic range, the matter of matter becomes strange indeed. Instead of infinitesimal fragments of indisputable tangibility, the inhabitants of the extreme microcosm are creatures of force, charge, frequency, spin, and even more exotic, abstract properties such as *flavor* and *color*.

Matter *is* what energy *does*. The progress of physics, a field once called simply "natural philosophy," has been the story of penetrating the mysteries of existence, or attempting to do so, by quantifying shifting sands in perpetual motion, tracing vibrations of information generated in matrices of relation.

Poetry, of course, has been pursuing this inquiry since the dawn of organized language, using tools of imagery, analogy and legend to portray patterns of cyclical recurrence.

We frequently labor under an embedded tendency, particularly in the traditions of Western thought, to view time as a linear progression, as a marker steadily and doggedly pushing the primitive past toward the progressing future, dragging all of us along with it.

Our timepieces faithfully record this consistent motion, as we collectively lurch toward advancing hours, later dates, and numerically superior years. We keep our walls cluttered with clocks and calendars, synchronized in order to symbolize this absolute temporal reality, often forgetting that these units of time represent a return to previous celestial positions as much as a progression forward from them.

The resurgence of cycles are a rare source of reliability in an often uncomfortably unpredictable set of ordered Chaos. The dependable repetition of dawn, day, dusk, and darkness anchors our subjective experiences to common reference points, albeit arbitrarily.

As creatures bred on these periods, it seems natural to be constantly segmenting slices of life, codifying consciousness as a creature of duration, spooned out in bite-sized reflections of Terran rotation and revolution.

Systems for reckoning time are as basic to cultures

as language, cuisine, and mythology. It is not inconsequential that most formal calendars are strictly regulated by various religious traditions, or that each large-scale franchise of theology sports its own branded version.

In this fashion, minds are synchronized to follow specialized datebooks, kept on the same page, unifying communities through observance of ritual obligations.

The Earth, however, does not pause in rotation to celebrate the passing of a day, nor does it halt in solar orbit to commemorate the transition to a new year. What we call nightfall is a relentless curtain of Sun-shadow spreading across the globe, an encroaching eclipse caused by interference from the planet itself.

Despite conventions of chronology, modern scales of travel and communication have made clear that *when* and *where* are highly interrelated, co-dependent concepts, making it more coherent to speak of spatial and temporal identities in terms of each other, all ways in motion.

The *Gyroscape* is my way of thinking about the universal matrix of motion, powered by the momentum of intersecting vectors in dynamic equilibrium states. This particular pattern appears to be inherent in all processes, mirrored in each phase of animation within space and time. The following lyrics are largely hymns to this harmony, the source and force of life itself.

The occupations and preoccupations of the theoretical scientist and the literary artist overlap in this contemplation of being and becoming. The key difference is that scientists are responsible for the *verifiability* of their findings, whereas writers are responsible for the *veracity* of them.

Rhythms of respiration, infusion and exhalation, the circulation of new and old blood, beat by the pulsing pump at the heart of physical embodiment, depict an ongoing event on which every cell depends. So it is with the breath of fresh perspectives; the flow must go on.

Language serves as a conduit for the transfer of consciousness. Speech is directed breath, the sharing of selected thoughts converted into sounds, integrated into the immediate reaction of our neighbors. Dynamic and largely lost in the instant, such words fade fast, and are therefore cheap, unless they are recorded and preserved.

More rarely, guided hands tap out coded thoughts, launching them in a state of suspended animation, to be received and interpreted at a later date by a wide variety of eyes. Such projected communication may be called *scripture*, *history*, or *literature*, but in any case represents a bridge to distant minds separated by chronology and location.

Sometimes, a work of writing is brought to the stage, reborn as a repeating element of speech or song. Live music on stage is a type of theater, a model of consciousness, melodic stories flowing through energetic circuits and dispersing to those in attendance. At the end of the night, the songs belong to the audience.

Which brings us to the present moment, a convergence of experience between us, you and I, which is *being* initiated as I type this self-referential sentence, and *becoming* consummated by your reading of it at some future point.

This page is manifesting *now*, but the day and date assigned to this particular instant will markedly differ for each of us. Books are time machines, linking us across the ages.

These are messages in a bottle, on a strange path toward musical adaptation, hurtling toward you from my little desert isle into an ocean of unknown currents. I do not know the destinations of these carefully selected words, but I trust they will wash up wherever you are, whoever you may be, and whenever your version of *now* happens to pass.

Welcome to my spin on the Universe. I do hope you're comfortable here. Things get a little *meta* sometimes, if you know what I mean.

-ASAOS Hx3
Indi Riverflow

Dharma Map

I went to see the guru
To score some destiny
Just enough to tide me through
'Til I could fix my color TV

Said to me you must be new
For I have seen you before
And if you truly had a clue
You'd back right out that door

But we'll toss darts at the chart
If you've nothing else to do
Maybe you'll start to fall apart
Maybe get hooked on the glue

Freedom found
In the heart of the trap
We're homeward bound
The long way round
All wrapped up
In our Dharma maps

I sat baffled in the tiny shrine
It wasn't quite what I'd had in mind
No signs of any grand design
Indeed no lines of any kind

o

I tried to take it all in stride
But I didn't know what to think
Was I being taken for a ride
Or was the map in invisible ink?

Said maybe this you'll understand
You venture into unknown lands
So don't ask me what's the plan
The way is drawn by your own hand

Freedom found
In the heart of the trap
We're homeward bound
The long way round
All wrapped up
In our Dharma maps

Invert Rarity

I collect impossibilities
And other pure fantasies
I have antidotes for gravity
And many cures for reality

I once thought I was wrong
Turned out I was mistaken
Didn't take too very long
To see that Fate was only fakin'

The stamp of invert rarity
In a desert of spare hilarity
The glitch which can switch polarity
An error you'd never dare correct
Quite the opposite of what you'd expect

Slipping on stepping stones
Dripping from dangerous streams
Cascading over cliffs of unknowns
Careening into sordid dreams

No wealth can purchase poverty
Hard-won scrawlings on the walls
The very scarcest commodities
Simply can't be bought at all

Nothing can be more precious
Than unvarnished veracity
The richest pearls are priceless
Beyond the grasp of mortality

The stamp of invert rarity
In a desert of spare hilarity
The glitch which can switch polarity
An error you'd never dare correct
Quite the opposite of what you'd expect

Existential Roulette

Been in suspended animation
Running real-world simulations
Of quasi-conscious creations
In disorganized formations

Forecast calls for unreasonably
High degrees of unpredictability
Unfounded rumors of plausibility
With a chance of partial absurdity

I can't lose this wager
Cause I'm not in it to win it
I'm an odd sort of player
I'm only in it to spin it

I'm betting on wild speculation
A rapid decline in inflation
The permanence of transition
Constantly shifting positions

The paradox of any paradigm
Is there's no way to not waste time
In a world so well past its prime
Running out of beanstalks to climb

I can't lose this wager
Cause I'm not in it to win it
I'm an odd sort of player
I'm only in it to spin it

I've been studying contradictions
With utterly detached devotion
I've come to the obvious conclusion
That truth is just a form of confusion

I'll bet I was born in plenty of debt
Ante bound to be perpetually unmet
But that has never stopped me yet
At the wheel of existential Roulette

I can't lose this wager
Cause I'm not in it to win it
I'm an odd sort of player
I'm only in it to spin it

Blast Dynamics

There was a moment of silence
And all existence quite frozen
Then the primordial suspense
Abruptly found itself broken
Splintered in horizon events
Thundered dimensions awoken
Flashpoint ripples of radiance
Sparking pyrotechnic explosions

Panning the grand panoramic
In the dust of blast dynamics
Putting energy into entropy
Sorting signals out of static

Quivering of superstrings
Pouring forth Kundalini
Magic acts attracting rings
Around magnetic Houdinis
Tapping vortex wellsprings
From the deep source of things
Multiplying and electrifying
Amplifying and magnifying

Panning the grand panoramic
In the dust of blast dynamics
Putting energy into entropy
Sorting signals out of static

Along the scale of vibrations
Composing harmony's home
Each spans a range of operations
Converging at the point of Om
Breathing seeds of invocation
Focused undivided intention
Cast with sense of consequence
And a vision of invention

Less Epic

I got something up my sleeve
A trick which will drop your jaw
So slick it'll bend what you believe
And have you question what you saw
Once you've seen a giant rabbit
Pull wizards from a black top hat
The only conclusion left to draw
Is this might be sanity's last straw

I've got a kettlepot cooking
Whipping up a messy recipe
Of holiness and sin
All I've perceived
And all I have been
All I've attempted
And all I've achieved
It's less epic than you'd imagine
And more amazing than you'd believe

I keep wonders under my hat
Ancient secrets studded in trust
Scribbled oracles folded flat
Ironies encrusted with rust

Poor prophets try to tell what's true
When vision is all in angle of view
We're all doing what we must
Before our stories disperse to dust

I hear the pulsing of my heart
Golden age on the stage unveiled
Triggered by the state of the start
And all the art we have inhaled
Driven by a deep desire to give
A present to all who dare to live
The epic tale of how we prevailed
And the less epic tale of how we failed

I've got a kettlepot cooking
Whipping up a messy recipe
Of holiness and sin
All I've perceived
And all I have been
All I've attempted
And all I've achieved
It's less epic than you'd imagine
And more amazing than you'd believe

All Due Electricity

Hunting out the words between the words
Listening for visions crying to be heard
It's a mission measured in melody
Wholeness, integrity and clarity

Does it glimmer shimmer in the mist
Evoking passion like a teenager's kiss?
Will it strike the soul like a typewriter key
From the first half of the last century?

Will the syllables hold what I meant to convey?
Does it make any sense if I put it this way?
Will anyone care what I have to say
In the peculiar mood I am lost in today?

Right now we hear a boom of choices
Selected serenely from a roomful of voices
With all due electricity
Here's the story
Of how this moment came to be

The way is paved, but the path is rough
Are these lines too bold, or not enough?
Does it slide smoothly off the cuff
Or fly away in a cloud of fluff?

Fit the flood in fresh new frames
Which somehow fail to sound the same
Call these sensations by a name
Playing pin-the-tail language games

Currents carry waves of energy
All we know is the front of the flow
Stringing along songs of synergy
Wherever motion is able to go

Right now we hear a boom of choices
Selected serenely from a roomful of voices
With all due electricity
Here's the story
Of how this moment came to be

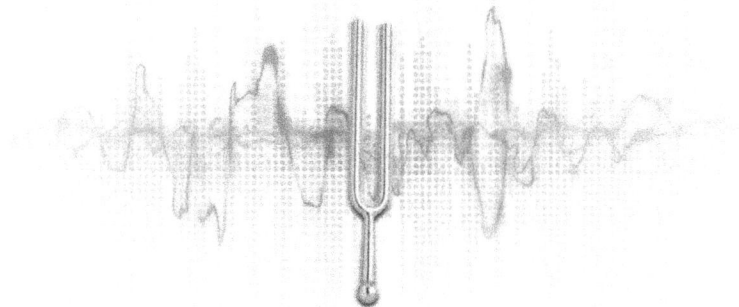

Rorschach Cadillac

Some Rorschach Cadillac
Rolled into the bivouac
With doors of golden guitars
I flipped through all the almanacs
Scanning forecasts like a maniac
But there are no types of cars
Only pictures made of stars
Listed in the Zodiac

Call it intuition
Call it premonition
Call it whatever you like
Call it divination
Or the mind's own creation
The future's calling you
For an encore lightning strike

Got a little bit tipsy
So I went to see the gypsy
To learn what lay ahead
Shuffled cards very stiffly
Then she counted to fifty
And got out some jam to spread
Said I'll be back in a jiffy
And if you're feeling kinda iffy
Here's your chance to dance in bed

Call it intuition
Call it premonition
Call it whatever you like
Call it divination
Or the mind's own creation
The future's calling you
For an encore lightning strike

Blew out all my fuses
And I left it to the Muses
Wrapped up in a cloud to wait
They ran me through ruses
Exposed all the excuses
And sent me to meet my fate
As speckled light diffuses
Not quite sure what the news is
But I bet it's gonna sound great

Call it intuition
Call it premonition
Call it whatever you like
Call it divination
Or the mind's own creation
The future's calling you
For an encore lightning strike

Partner Ship

A palace built in quicksand
Only has so long to stand
While sunlit skies glow
And fair-weather winds blow

Soon enough storms will show
That's when we'll really know
If there's any solid foundation
Or just a hasty imagination

The hardest part of Partner Ship
Is settling on one course
When we're all on a different trip
Back to the same old source

Some crave commands of royalty
I'd rather live in lands of loyalty
Oh, I'd let roomfuls of treasure rust
Just to cover my back in slack and trust

Cutting keys to communication
Keeping equality in the equation
Selecting a collective direction
Where our paths find connection

The hardest part of Partner Ship
Is settling on one course
When we're all on a different trip
Back to the same old source

Sometimes I come on too strong
Other times perhaps too meek
And if we never risk being wrong
Then we will truly be too weak

The confusion we chance
In improvising our dance
Charting new frames of reference
Taking dominion out of deference

Road I Ride

The road I ride
Isn't marked on any map
It's a little off to the side
From where pandas lay their traps
Out where outlaws hide
The tunnels are where I reside
A little dirt I take in stride
No room for undue pride
On the road I ride

The road I ride
Is made up day to day
And I wouldn't be bona fide
If I claimed I knew the way
Guesses are my only guide
It gets pretty cut-and-dried
Not a whole lot to decide
Whatever's not denied
Is the road I ride

The road I ride
Designed for great and small
And if I may confide
It's not fit for walking tall
You can go the whole world wide
Where no wall can divide
The real trip goes on inside
Magic demystified
That's the road I ride

The road I ride
Isn't for the feint of art
The only end implied
Is returning where it starts
I can only say that I have tried
To collect what coincides
For all who simply won't abide
Too slick to let it slide
That's the road I ride

The road I ride
Defined by obstacles
And cannot be classified
By make of any vehicle
Sometimes I'm clear Shang-haied
Or chased out by the roaring tide
Providence always provides
Aphorisms get applied
Along the road I ride

The road I ride
An avenue through space
Visible to the wild-eyed
With some answers to chase
Sometimes strange ideas collide
I like reality deeply fried
Half a step from certified
Banging on old ironside
That's the road I ride

Nips Of Honesty

Seems beyond self-evident
That it would've been smart
To get in front of this moment
Right from the start
Lots of lines that fell face-flat
But we gotta get past that

At times I may be too direct
For polite diplomacy
Protecting truth from neglect
In the airs of courtesy
Time ain't planning on sitting pat
But we gotta get past that

I'm not nearly as angry
As I may appear to be
The chill you feel is only
Wind-whipped nips of honesty
I've run clean out of diplomat
And we gotta get past that

Brisk words can come in raw
Slicing paper-thin skin
When this glacier finally thaws
You'll see how timid we've been
We'll top out the thermostat
And we'll get past that

The truth can be cold
So we wrap ourselves in lies
But if I may be so bold
I'm tired of wearing a disguise
Piece of mind hiding under my hat
Half past time to get past that

Jack of Knacks

I'm a painter with sounds
Mechanic of totaled hearts
Conductor of cut-up clowns
And fluent in six tongues of art

Born ready for a Renaissance
In an age of science fiction
A creature created by a world of wants
Where the best lack all conviction

They say it's written in the Will
That the meek shall inherit the Earth
Let's get that page to probate court
Before another bomb gives birth

I've got eyes on the back of my back
Always on point to take up the slack
I'm a jack of all knacks
Master of hacks
On the wrong track
Slipping through all the right cracks

My leaders were mostly liars
So I sought the self-evident
Sparking fires in live wires
With drive-by enlightenment

Knee-deep in ruins as I trace
Eroded signs left behind
Puzzle pieces into place
Guessing my best and reckoning blind

I'm the very modular
Modern major generalist
Bringing in to being
Whatever needs to exist
My specialty is adaptability
And the will to persist
On a wave of creativity
No fortress can resist

The Magician

The wizard in an amber robe
Reeling from astral realms he probes
Twisting the system half insane
Rivers of symbols in intricate chains

Some might try to call it sorcery
This mutual conspiracy
Of suspicious serendipity
But the juggler only laughs
Behind the shroud of secrecy
Stands a lifetime of craft

If you read between the lines
The prism'd path begins to shine
The energy runs warm and cool
Summoned from a vast and empty pool
What a flow when the pump is primed
Persistence trumps genius every time

Delighting in slight of mind
Lighting patterns of illuminated design
Adept in all the empyrean arts
Unsure where he ends and eternity starts

All these arts are claimed to deceive
Held together with whatever web we weave
Uniting illusions we barely believe
The half-deck shuffle with rabbit in sleeve
But magic hides under the belly of sham
Bursting dams with battering rams

If you read between the lines
The prism'd path begins to shine
The energy runs warm and cool
Summoned from a vast and empty pool
What a flow when the pump is primed
Persistence trumps genius every time

When the rebel son arrived with his staff
Tired of splitting wheat from chaff
The Pharaoh's court and wizards gasped
For it was a serpent's tail he grasped

The halls of the pyramids
Rang with incantations and spells
The walls of the pyramids
Glyphs graven where dynasties dwell
The fall of the pyramids
From the apex of heaven to the pit of hell
The call of the pyramids
Ringing through the ages like an unbroken bell

Locksmiths
For Ann and Sasha Shulgin

There's buried treasure
Forgotten and hidden
Maps to pleasures
Long forbidden
Means to measure
Myriad dimensions
And blueprints for cultures
Awaiting invention

No one knows what shines inside
This gold that shows
What our blinders hide
Only that it glows
Like the torch of stellar guides
Sparking up the Zodiac
When a star's giving birth
With the force of a thundercrack
At the dawn of Earth

Can we bear to stare
At the Universe undressed?
We can only guess
Unless we are free
If this fire lights the way
Or burns our eyes
Displays the truth
Or a new set of lies

Rogue locksmiths tinkering
With secrets of alchemy
Testing ring after ring
Of untried molecular keys
Exploring the underbelly
Of cosmic chemistry

The heart's wild hackers
And the soul's safe-crackers
All want inside this vault
But there's always some sentry
Guarding every entry
Waving guns and crying halt

Shelves of strange potions
Born of chemical devotion
In the lab where many kinds
Of magical logic combine
Unlocking the mind's design
One atom at a time

Together they ventured
Beneath the neural firmament
Detailing each experiment
Meticulous and miraculous
Tracking lost passages
To the catacombs of bliss

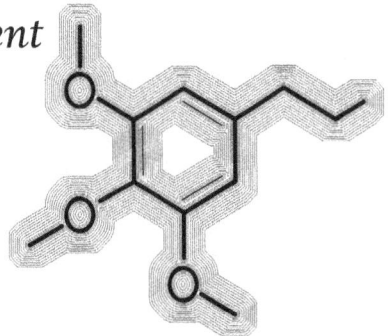

Smuggling Smoke

Standby for the catch-phrase king
Hanging on to his high by a very thin string
Superhero quick and Houdini slick
As white rabbits leap from his bag of tricks

As a cloud of glitter spun the room
Sustained by a psychic sonic boom
Till dawn's early darkness shone
On how big and bad your pride had grown

Once I thought you were the Devil himself
With Heaven in a bottle sitting right on your shelf
When the Reaper arrives to ring your bell
Bet you'll turn a profit smuggling smoke into Hell

The very best and worst of friends
Vowed to back me till the bitter end
Filled to the brim with vinegar and piss
Guess I always knew it would go down like this

We danced to summon acid rain
We drove blindly in the fastest of lanes
We'd pray to melt the world away
Shuffling in shadows to keep our sight at bay

In the highway haze I missed the signs
The turnoff to madness you decided we'd drive
Gambling our flesh along the double line
As if you were trying to get out of staying alive

Once I thought you were the Devil himself
With Heaven in a bottle sitting right on your shelf
When the Reaper arrives to ring your bell
Bet you'll turn a profit smuggling smoke into Hell

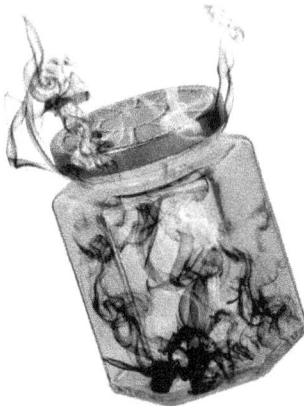

It's all about timing
And being where it's at
When the temperature is climbing
Bust out the welcome mat
Teapot whistle
Mercury's gone to your head
Everybody scramble
Hatter's mad
And seeing red

Once I thought you were the Devil himself
With Heaven in a bottle sitting right on your shelf
When the Reaper arrives to ring your bell
Bet you'll turn a profit smuggling smoke into Hell

Rule of RAW

For Robert Anton Wilson, the imaginary writer.

The science of synchronicity
Gratuitous fortuitous serendipity
It's all that and a bushel of flax
House of cards and house of wax

Twenty-three ways to connect the dots
Pattern is there even when it's not
What you look for is what you get
Each coin flip is a well-hedged bet
You'll be on the side you probably survived
Good things always come in fives

Schrödinger's hypothetical pet cat
Tortured cruelly in the name of math
The quantum hairballs immediately flew
Whole lotta crow swallowed over that cat's mu

Cat said, yeah, I've got your answer
Been working at it for a while
It's yes and no and maybe or
Both and neither by your style

Twenty-three ways to connect the dots
Pattern is there even when it's not
What you look for is what you get
Each coin flip is well-hedged bet
You'll be on the side you probably survived
Good things always come in fives

More than one way to yin a cat
Or pull it out of a trick-top hat
You're the only one keeping score
Maybe you're the Bob you've been waiting for

Crossing the Rubicon

It's the plot of a book
And you're living on pages
Everywhere you look
Trapped in Tristero's traces

Is it some twisted hoax
Or a warped hallucination
Shadows wrapped in cloaks
Fleeing with your imagination

Truth's a many-headed hydra
Every answer has a twin
There isn't any box big enough
To squeeze the Universe in

Might be a digital analogy
A most authentic imitation
Some common peculiarity
From rainbows of gravitation

Spherical symmetries
Forming and breaking
Around parallel polarities
Of dreaming and waking

We've crossed the Rubicon
And now the die is cast
Laser-razed lost lexicons
Illuminate the hidden past

Truth's a many-headed hydra
Every answer has a twin
There isn't any box big enough
To squeeze the Universe in

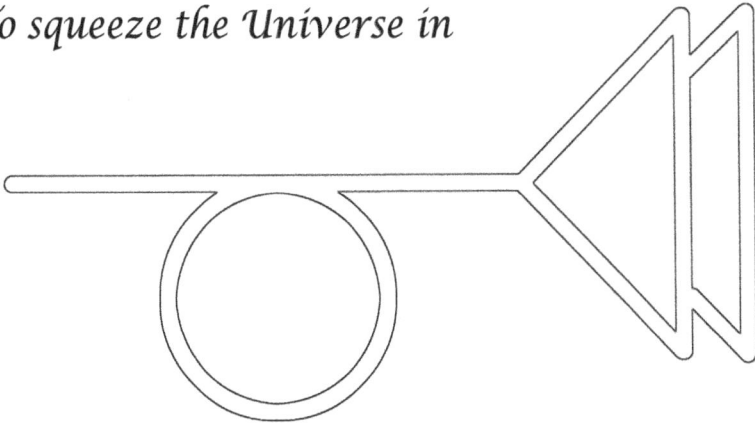

Simplicity

There is nothing quite as sweet
As the beauty of a breath
Nor sour as our common defeat
The final gasp of ashen death

With this air so abundantly rare
Our time to taste it slipping away
I swear we have no more to spare
Indulging this fighting today

Our views align in unity
Somewhere between one and infinity
A precise point in complexity
Picked by the click of simplicity

Pandora's treasure is a clever trap
Opening up a million more gaps
Never mind fiddling with locks
It's time to think around the box

Truth is an estimation
As obvious as it is obscure
We're in it for the duration
So we may as well endure

Our views align in unity
Somewhere between one and infinity
A precise point in complexity
Picked by the click of simplicity

No crisis ever could be so great
That quibbling won't make it worse
Waste this space in endless debate
With winds which won't reverse

Peace presents the golden riddle:
Where do opposite sides agree?
Truth might be right down the middle
Halfway between you and me

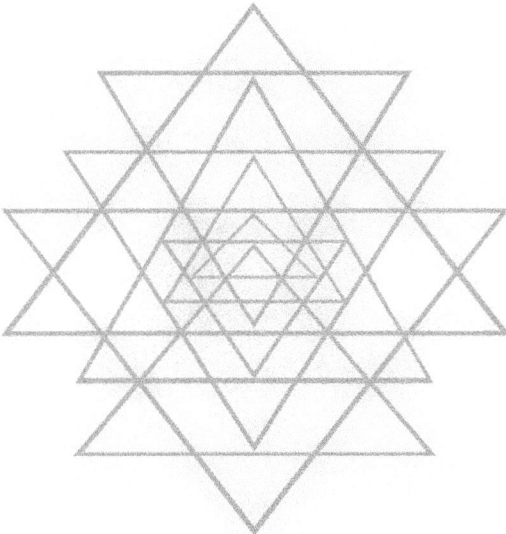

Optimal

Pointed on a narrow line
The way may seem so clear
Cling to vainglorious vines
Or fall in briartraps of fear

But one day the slant of light
Shines on just the right spot
Triggers in the nerves a second sight
Where the curves connect the dots

It is all impossible up until
It has become inevitable
Energy is the primal animal
Ever hunting out the optimal

Upon rare reflection
Turns out the world is round
And therefore any direction
May well be homeward bound

And now the lines do appear
To weave circles and spiral knots
And these are merely parts of spheres
We aren't sure yet how to plot

It's a volatile volley
Across the recurring years
Fueled by streams of fiery folly
And plenty of grit in the gears

It is all impossible up until
It has become inevitable
Energy is the primal animal
Ever hunting out the optimal

Key Of Now

There is language which is spoken
Giving breath to gasping thoughts
Sent on rafts of air as tokens
To return what time has taught

Some ideas find the mind smitten
Words worthy of another look
With desperation these are written
Born to bodies of fine-lined books

Always after more of what passed before
Grasping to catch some life from the dead
Making memories into metaphors
Spun from pale parable threads

Wisdom comes in many tongues
Many ways to use the air in our lungs
Many ways to link the old to young
But few ring as true
As the truth that is sung

The particle points to here on the map
The wave is the way it fills the gap
All we can know is the world as it was
Matter is what energy does

George Brown died on Friday
Caged by cadence and chord
Chromatic calligraphy
The inner face of space explored

Spotter calls out for land
Hanging from the bow
But it's just a note of sand
Written in the Key of Now

Wisdom comes in many tongues
Many ways to use the air in our lungs
Many ways to link the old to young
But few ring as true
As the truth that is sung

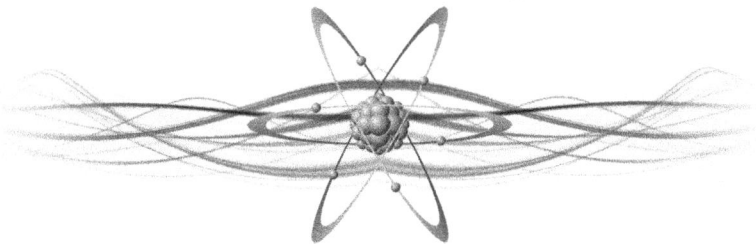

Reset

High mojo in the hole
Heavy spells getting sprung
From the bottom of my soul
To the tip of my tongue

It's been quite a blast
Still ringing in my ears
One last call for the past
Coming through loud and clear

Who I've been is wearing thin
Serpent shedding another skin
Go ahead, hit the reset button
And start all over again

Farewell you forlorn fantasies
Dreams from disappearing years
Lose the you who used to be
Slip into a brand new gear

Shells of selves chipped away
Collapsing walls within
Clearing out all the yesterday
So tomorrow can now begin

Chrysalis burst asunder
We've opened up the sky
My, it's cracking with thunder
That would be my cue to fly

Who I've been is wearing thin
Serpent shedding another skin
Go ahead, hit the reset button
And start all over again

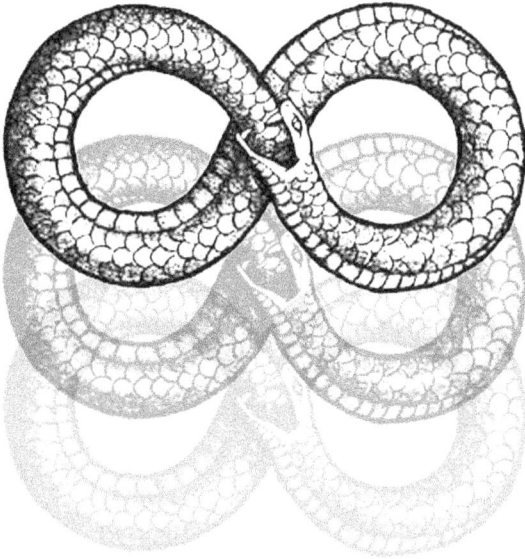

Desert Trance
Music by John Kadlecik
First performed by JKB 9-2-11

Sky was raining question marks
Spirits spinning bodies of dust
Air rippling with cobalt sparks
Finding new life with each new gust

Coming to in a bed of thorns
Beneath a scalding hot pink dome
The wailing wind imitating horns
Mirages curdling up with foam

A crowd appeared like smoke
Where nothing at all should be
Wondered just what kind of joke
The desert was playing on me

Time to make it happen
Just like we done before
Yes, it's time to make it happen
Time to open up that door

The ambrosia and the nectar flowed
Lost all track of time
After a while everything glowed
Beyond reason or rhyme

Mobius band got out of hand
A bearded giant sat up on a cliff
Smile so wide it lit up the land
As he teased a familiar riff

Time to make it happen
Just like we done before
Yes, it's time to make it happen
Shake things to the core

Goatman Pan with a pipe and a plan
Playin' Bacchanalian Jam
Looping distortions through the caves
Building castles out of waves

Sarasvati strumming slide sitar
Seven sisters down from the stars
Sitting in as a backup choir
Pele dancing and breathing fire

Shiva rocking skins with all six limbs
Beating upon singularity's rim
Drumming out the dead in single file
Chugging Soma like it's going out of style

Gyroscape

We awoke to timeless void
Stirred by echoes of when
Worlds were born and destroyed
Eye spun wide once again
But there was no view to see
So we exploded with curiosity

Gyroscape whipped in a whirl
The world is your oyster
But don't swallow the pearl
Motion is what matters
Patterns create and deviate
Set in constantly dynamic states

Particles and planets
Dance in a ring
Swung through space
On an invisible string
Wanting what is lacked
Sliding on a track
Propelling
Every
Single
Thing

Spin on spin on
Rocks on a roll
Cruisin' for a fusion
With no particular goal
Movin' and groovin'
Around parallaxis poles
Spin on spin on spin on

Turning circuits reel-to-real
We're caught in gaps of gears
Carried away by days and years
Mer-ka-ba blazing fiery light
Fueling the furnace out of sight
Chariots in celestial flight

Beating with Brahma's breath
Born on the heels of death
Sparks fade as flames appear
Stars burn out and shift career
Dreamer awakens stirred and shaken
Reborn to remind nothing's mistaken

For every revolution
Is bursting with change
In constant rotation
Awaiting the strange
Holograms engaged
In energy exchange
Each cycle the same
Just uniquely arranged

Cosmic song composed
In the wind of swirling spheres
The common core exposed
And the connections are clear
All ways in motion but going nowhere

Clockwork

These are our hands
Counting grains of sand
Splitting infinity into bits
Which we can understand

And here are the gears
Where the cycle appears
Eternally returning
Hours to months and years

Now here is your moment
The last one was spent
This instant flashes past
Wondering where it went
Clicking away like clockwork
Capturing seconds of every event

Springing into being
As the pendulum swings
Alternating extremes
Plucking cosmic strings

Choreography of quarks
Spectacle of dancing sparks
From momentum of drums
Beating in the distant dark

Now here is your moment
The last one was spent
This instant flashes past
Wondering where it went
Clicking away like clockwork
Capturing seconds of every event

$E=MC^2$

We spring from the oil of the ocean
Strings gifted with strange locomotion
Waving our dirty laundry in the air
In case anyone really cares
Measuring success by the shadows we cast
Seeding the future and grading the past
Preparing for what no one's ever prepared
Energy equals mind times consciousness squared

Each breath is part of the conspiracy
Awash in a shower of electricity
Trying to become what we already are
Inside the womb it's tough to see
But we're sitting on a star
Sitting on a star

We gather with the motive of motion
Bound to the spiral of devotion
Saying life isn't real and life isn't fair
Wondering why in the hell we are here
Measuring success in instants of yes
Caught in a loop of infinite regress
The slow are slain, the quick are spared
Evolution equals memory times change squared

Spark of inversion
Catalytic conversion
Photons streaming in
On a gust of solar wind
Nursing on light and second sight
Stuck in the cold night
Till we get it right

You may not believe me
But we are bound to go far
This waterlogged age
Just the embryonic stage
In the life cycle of a star

We brew ourselves from a pot of potion
Generated by heat of emotion
Vying to ensnare a match for our pair
An opposite with which to share
Measuring success in units of happiness
Gambling the future on a whim and a guess
Leaving to legend how bravely we dared
Synergy equals magic times compassion squared

Spot of Mandelbrot

I am the model-maker
Replicating all of Nature
Rendering the big picture
Too expansive to capture
Delivering it in miniature

Every star becomes a dot
Each story told a small subplot
Just a spot of Mandelbrot
Flashing past in quick snapshots
Of scenes time long ago forgot

Blinking lonely nodes
Linking to the motherlode
Wading in the flow
Just waiting to go

Models are exhibitionist
Curving contours lightly kissed
Treating each eye to a tryst
Lingering on every little twist
Exposing more than I care to exist

Drawing the Universe to scale
Tracing snakes swallowing tails
Galaxies poured into grails
Recreating creation's trail
Down to the finest and last detail

Blinking lonely nodes
Linking to the motherlode
Wading in the flow
Just waiting to go

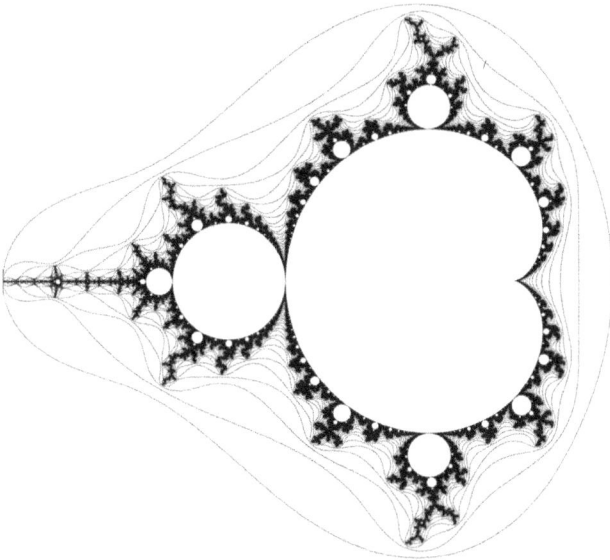

Set Of Jewels

Sapphire locket wrapped on a spire
Flames licking out at the edge of fire
Insane indeed, but only north by northwest
It can be predicted but never guessed

She's a complex girl with a simple rule
Every appendage must be encrusted with jewels
Hair of every color, flesh of every tone
There's no style she does not make her own

Julia my love how you hold my gaze
I could stare at your splendors for a thousand days
Never to master your infinite maze
Never fully understanding your ways

Each second with her brings a surprise
As she changes the hue of alien skies
Study her face, tracing what is shown
Right before your eyes another has grown

She treads on a bed of snowflakes
Jet-skis splashing along nebula wakes
Branches splitting off from her shoulders
Trailing planets, pebbles and boulders

Recursively riding on a seahorse tail
Hiding beneath the shell of a snail
Driven by an engine which uses no fuel
Persisting in a state of constant renewal

Elf in Self
Inside pockets
I sighed I sighed
Massed misty mysteries
Murmuring murmuring
Morphing morphing
More less more less
Meaning meaning
Less more less more
Morphemes morphemes
More wispy memories
Murmuring murmuring
Our ride our ride
Outside sockets
Similar
To Self

What does golden mean to you?
Living geometry always breeds true
The rate at which the Universe grew
The blueprint for order Chaos drew

Models and monuments cast from the die
Spirals and circles ruled by pi and phi
On a mission to eternally reiterate
The pattern she's bound to replicate

The Source

I sing yesterday's refrains
As I dream tomorrow's tunes
Scrying my soul
Like a scattered plate of runes
Seeking new ways to praise
The beauty of the moon
Sliver of silver painted by night
Carved and filled in endless phase
Content to share the light
From the Source's glorious rays

Hit land as a castaway tossed from sea
Wet behind the ears and weak in the knees
Grasping at fruit from every tree
Praying this one will teach what it means to be me
All these mirrors reflecting strange faces
Shuffling for places in diminishing spaces

There was an instant
When it all came crystal clear
The center is now
We enter it here

Each day we play
The journey of the year
The mountain melting
Beneath fire rain pelting

Setting the water on its course
River swelling and winding
Each drop finding
Its way back to the Source

Met three pilgrims on a quest to the East
Barefoot and baying and burdened like beasts
Following the sunrise toward holy ground
Where the gates to Paradise might be found
One sought by breath, and one by eyes
And one by death to be free of lies

I too once climbed to caves of ice
The master graced me with a bag of rice
As I descended weary from the hike
Beset by beggars and hustlers alike
I pressed in each palm a sacred grain
All strength drained was slowly regained
Like the sky must feel to offer Earth rain

The gift is in the giving
My way of thanking you for living
I'd just as soon that you have the blessing
For we're all the same light
In different dressing
We might push to the front by force
But only as One
May we return to the Source

Manifest Station

Did you ever stop to wonder
Who scattered this trail of silver?
And crafted rafts to save
Some unknown child of the river?
We knew you'd one day crest this wave
A dreamer and a giver
This stream is bubbling with treasures
Only visible to the brave
Who trust us to deliver

We can conjure what you crave
It works as well without a wand
The power is in the wave
And a little help from the great beyond
Count the shells you've saved
If you trust your motivation
Just redeem your blessings
On the way to Manifest Station

We're beckoned by the echo of laughter
Summoned by levity's elevation
You won't find what you're after
In any book of incantations
Orient on whatever makes you whole
That's your destination
Bring your body mind and soul
Together at Manifest Station

Let's get this wish
To Manifest Station
The electric express
To Manifest Station
No need to guess
About Manifest Station
Go East Go West
To Manifest Station
Just bring your best
To Manifest Station

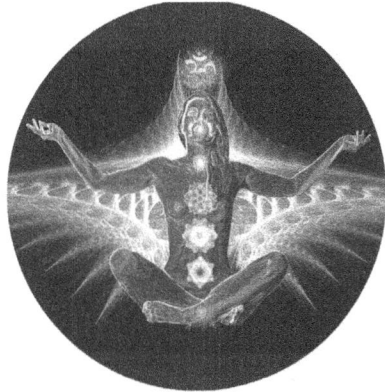

Karma Wheel

There are many rides in this carnival
Roller coasters in perpetual festival
Dark houses haunted by greed and guilt
Parades of giant rulers stalking on stilts
Dunk tanks where someone soaks when you win
Pirate planks where you walk off your sin
And halls of mirrors where you talk to your twin

We'll be whizzing by at the speed of why
In the land that lies beyond the lie
I'll try on a new view of you for size
Borrowing everyone else's eyes
Karma's just an abstraction
Until you see it in action

It can be so hard to see the me in you
On the other end of what we do
It's never real until you feel
The flip side of the Karma Wheel

To those that fed my hunger a meal
To all the petty tyrants and real big deals
To all the hustlers hunting souls to steal
The drones who called my dreams unreal
And teachers who gave me the tools to heal
I'll see you all on the Karma Wheel

It can be so hard to see the me in you
On the other end of what we do
It's never real until you feel
The flip side of the Karma Wheel

The boomerang comes 'round again
Circling to hit the hand hate bends
Sooner or later we face familiar stares
In the carnival of contrast and compare
Fair play makes for a merry go-around
Glares shot at mirrors are bound to rebound
We all must swim in the sea of our sounds

Hall of a Million Mirrors

I ventured into a hall
Of a million mirrors
Where I beheld the set of all
Bent by grace of place
In space and years
A panorama of possibilities
The face of every conceivable me

I saw every deviation
The worst and the best
Recursive iterations
Lives of the lowliest
And most exalted stations
Artists and hustlers
Hawking innovation

Sat Nam
Sa Ta Na Ma
Sat Narayan Wha He Guru
Hari Narayan
Sat Nam

I call myself to the Truth
Infinite cycle of being and becoming
Oceans of veracity and ecstasy
Unending circuit of creativity
I am the set of all I am

There were toilers and spoilers
Builders and destroyers
Fascination traders
In a ring of surface slickers
Imaginary paraders
Dancing in little flickers

The profligate and the vain
The methodically mad
And pathologically sane
Profiteers of war
And souls who fell before
Their inner monster
Drunk and thirsty for more

Saint and sinner
All stood at the door
Clad in robes of the rich
And rags of the poor
I opened up and let them in
All these versions of me
Who might have never been

Let's Bring the Healing

This palace is quickly losing luster
The courtyard's cluttered
Broken windows shuttered
Echoing every curse
That was ever muttered
Every misplaced word
That hate has uttered

This is a place with one-way doors
Where wealthy servants carefully ignore
Your protests as they steal all that is yours
And sell the furniture for a trifle more
This is a house that has forgotten the poor
We're not even sure what we built it for

The paint is peeling
On the sagging ceiling
Too much truth revealing
We're tired of kneeling
It's potluck planet and we plan on feasting

So let's bring the healing
Let's bring the healing

Let's invest in remodeling
Let's start by appealing
To that human feeling
We'll need more than a cosmetic change
The whole style must be rearranged

We've gotten so spun out on our polarities
We've misplaced half our humanity
Compassion is pure necessity
When we understand that I
am you
is we

So let's bring the healing
Let's bring the healing

Sick with worry
Sick with debt
Sick with doubt
Sick with regret
Sick with hatred
Sick inside out
Sick about what it's all about
Sick of dividing
Sick to the core
Sick of the mantra of more more more

Sick of lies raining from above
Sick of push and sick of shove
Sick even with too much love
Sick of always keeping score
And so very sick
Out of breath
Sick to death
Of this never-ending war
There's so much we're all sick of
So let's bring the healing

Xochipilli's Mask

Morning glory sacred smoke
Open the Sun
Inhale or choke
But never forget the way you woke
Peeling back the serpent's cloak

Standing by poets and the brave in battle
Armed with chants and dance
And shaking mad rattles
Panoramas carved into primal images
Taking tolls along astral bridges

They trek half the globe for a day of dream
Climb jungle cliffs and swim upstream
Just to shatter the story recited in vain
Heal psychic rifts and reset the brain

What you'd never seek is what you'll find
The root of the fruit
Of the divine
Wrestle with warrior tasks
Answer questions you tremble to ask
Be in the dance when you fall into trance
You gave it all for your chance to glance
At the visions behind
Xochipilli's mask

Some things can only be grasped
When the flower child has been unmasked

Mount pyramid steps the warrior's way
Source of sorcery shadows at play

Some things can only be grasped
When the flower child has been unmasked

Teonanácatl

Flesh of the Fifth
Excessive god
Eyes rolling back
Eternally awed

Some things can only be grasped
When the flower child has been unmasked

Quetzalcoatl

Step lightly on the serpent's tongue
Leaden feet are likely stung
Ladders latticed with invisible rungs
On which the heads of pretenders are hung

Nahautl

Languages lost
Cultures cost
Meet the new boss
Bearing a cross

Effigy unearthed
Inestimable worth
Totem of mirth
Calendar rebirth

Some things can only be grasped
When the flower child has been unmasked

Too Close To Call

This is where the elements combine
Where the green sheen
Meets the sunshine
Where energy greets
Matter's fine line

Hidden roots expand
Where we are unaware
Reflecting the span
Of rising canopy flares

Sometimes a rise looks like a fall
Sometimes a door comes off like a wall
You don't have to decide at all
You can call it too close to call

Some say it's all been scripted
That improv is an illusion
The stage directions are encrypted
So act out your own delusion

Truth is a floating point
Swinging on a swivel
Universal joint
Instant to instant spot to spot
Sifting stories and twisting plots

There is pretext and subtext
In a forest so immense
Once you've seen what's next
It all makes sense

Sometimes a rise looks like a fall
Sometimes a door comes off like a wall
You don't have to decide at all
You can call it too close to call

No matter what wit we profess
May as well just see
We're climbing a Tree
Knowing more and understanding less

I have no truth to tell you
Only a tale of verity
Best we can do is guess what's true
From shadows cast by the Tree

Sometimes a rise looks like a fall
Sometimes a door comes off like a wall
You don't have to decide at all
You can call it too close to call

On A Phrase

If you're testing my patience
I must say you've passed
I'll yield you the difference
If we can get over this fast

Bonfire zips
Beneath winter's glaze
We're only going through a phase
These days will slip
Into history's haze
If our bridge doesn't burn on a phrase

Memories we have spoiled
Clawing at each other's throats
The sacred ground we soiled
Stabbing Judas goats

Hairs split into pure thin air
Debating hallucinations
Scaling stairs which lead nowhere
In mindless reiteration

Seeds of hope
Beneath springtime rains
We were only going through a phase
Down slippery slopes
Over homegrown clichés
It always seems to turn on a phrase

Time is shaped like a funnel
Only one way to slide
Deeper in toward the tunnel
And out the other side

Just because we're here now
Doesn't mean we're not there then
There's a lot I'd love to disavow
But I'll probably do it all again

Fortune scorching
Under summer's rays
We're only going through a phase
We went torching
Set the Earth ablaze
Yesterday's ways return on a phrase

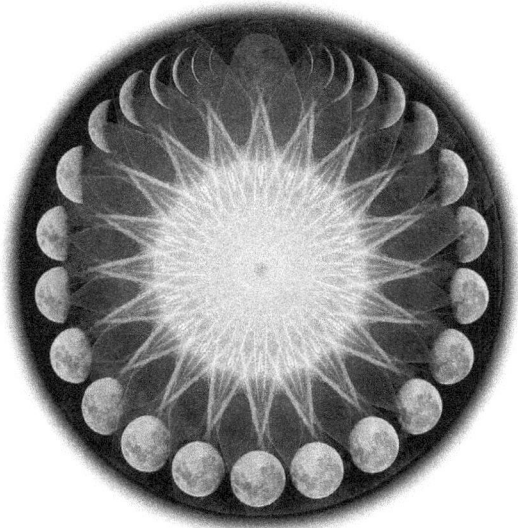

Own You Back

You may have yourself a gig
Where you dare not be late
A silver claim on which to dig
That now controls your fate
Chasing carrots and fleeing stress
Slaving for freedom and finding less

All these things which give you slack
Turn around and take it back
Mind's in a bind
And body's on loan
Who's tossing the bones?
Who is the owner, and who is owned?

Scrapbooks full of pale glories
All these stories you think are yours
Collecting another set of worries
And another set of chores
You might wonder what this game is for
And why one bothers keeping score

You may have set beliefs
That guide your every choice
Offering comfort and relief
In a soothing hypnotizing voice

Never imagining the worlds you've lost
On the straight arrow narrow path
If you knew what those easy answers cost
Heaven would be facing your wrath

You may even marshal armies
And tanks at your command
Warships flanking all the seas
And parading marching bands
Drumming up false loyalties
For all your brilliant plans

But when the lean and hungry
Crave the dominion in your hands
They'll cut you down just to be free
All your towers on all your land
Will devour your power and bury
Ozymandias where you stand

All these things which give you slack
Turn around and take it back
Mind's in a bind
And body's on loan
Who's tossing the bones?
Who is the owner, and who is owned?

Peephole

All I can remember
Is that I always forget
The timing of whatever
Hasn't happened yet

Drowning in duties
And tangled in debt
Dazzled by beauty
And hedging my bets

Hints of Oversoul
Poppin' through
Pairs of peepholes
Holy ghosts hosted
Among airy family trees
Teased out in synchronicity
Familiarities and similarities

Divining divine direction
Can be a dangerous task
Dividing truth into sections
Questions best unasked

Continents full of faults
The self in insurrection
Naked and unmasked
Quaking toward correction

Hints of Oversoul
Poppin' through
Pairs of peepholes
Holy ghosts hosted
Among airy family trees
Teased out in synchronicity
Familiarities and similarities

Tour's End

It's the end of tour now
We've come to the end of the line
But damn it worked out fine
One day when we rock in leisure
These pleasures we'll recall
Memory's precious treasures
Which make the trouble worth it all

We'll do it again in the pleasure domes
Though it's never quite the same
Land softly on memory's foam
With ghosts of roads we've roamed
Now we retreat to our various seats
And plan our next journey home

Racing full throttle
Stopped on a dime
Resetting each peak
To be the new baseline
On a race to redefine
What it means for a star to shine

All the hurdles we transcended
The stress test of delays
The tension that we tended
Maintaining a matrix of mainstays
Running out of fuel like a supersonic jet
Swallowing letters of the alphabet

Running through romances
Chasing that perfect pitch
And many chances for strange dances
Scratching at an irresistible itch
Driving down to the last battered ditch
In threads worn to the last tattered stitch

Making miles in sunshine smiles
Lost in the interstate city maze
Whistling all the while
Reality pierces through the haze
Spinning through our cranky dials
Yeah, these must be those good ole days

Fox In Sheep's Clothing
Written with Eric Olson of Hairball Willie

I conduct the half-hour of hate
A sock-puppet for the corporate state
Delivering a daily dose of fear
Of the enemies lurking far and near

There is no fact I will not slant
As I fill the air with self-righteous rants
My words wind their way to office and bar
Hypnotizing commuters as they steam in the car

My game is to redirect the blame
Reframe and defame with specious claims
Liberals or Muslims, it's all the same
Communists and terrorists by different names

I make the smoke to fill your screen
I'll wash your brain squeaky clean
I am the mouthpiece of the war machine
Turning blood red into American green

Wistful for Ike's black-and white golden age
When crew cuts and witch hunts were all the rage
Nuclear spread and apocalyptic dread
Feeding the monster under the bed

With wit as sharp as the point of an arrow
Keeping minds on the small and narrow
The masses wouldn't know what to think
If I weren't there between every drink

Hawking for progress back to the past
When the patriot's word was always the last
When women and races knew their places
And the market fell under God's good graces

I make the smoke to fill your screen
I'll wash your brain squeaky clean
I am the mouthpiece of the war machine
Turning blood red into American green

Boom and Bust

In the garden we gathered whatever we'd need
Till we were driven out by our insatiable greed
It was all over once the ape stood up straight
Lifted a hand to redefine fate
Couldn't see the forests for the wood
Confused by the fruiting body of evil and good

Echoes of the city of gold
Only heard in legends rarely told
Crumbled in battle pitting sun against moon
Scattered to the winds as we will be soon

Hand hammers windows with nails
Hoof that gets hammered plays and wails
One drunk on power, the other on wine
Staring at each other across the mind's fine line
One giving voice to the metal machine
The other the holiness of all that is green

Echoes of the city of silver
Set on the banks of the river
Fell to the ravages of riches in its prime
Heed it well, for history rhymes

Behold the Lord of Laws
The Lord of Lies
Lord that wants to poke out both your eyes
Binding the globe to one shadow of truth
Pulling freedom from every last rebellious tooth
Cursing the Devil seen in the mirror
Playing on panic at Nature's terrors

Echoes of the city of bronze
Built on the honor of warrior's bonds
Sacked by kings recovering a queen
Songs of heroes their bones picked clean

Citadels built on welted backs
Buried in silence beside the railroad tracks
Dreams dissolved in the Empire's grip
Hopes smashed with the flick of a whip

Layers of wool coiled into hangman's rope
Covering our eyes as we slip down the slope
What Providence will intervene to save
An Empire cursed by the suffering of slaves?

Spider queen weaving tapestry stitches
Backed by Her legion of dark-cloaked witches
Rising to raise a forest revival
Casting a circle for Earth's survival

Nearing the apex of the age of steel
Crushing the wild beneath our heel
We boom and we bust
But our towers are bound to rust
Now we decide if this will be the end
Or if golden times will dawn once again

Guarding the Garden

Flinching at the slightest sound
Where golden nuggets grow on trees
Sitting guard both ears to the ground
A pocketful of empty and a head full of needs

Eyes were bigger than your garden
Garden bigger than your dreams
Crisp icy nights it all starts to harden
It's never quite as easy as it seems
You know, never quite as easy as it seems

Tomorrow they'll be back shaking the skies
Swooping down with their whirlybird spies
Time melts to molasses, stars return my stare
One eye winks, but the other doesn't dare

Eyes were bigger than your garden
Garden bigger than your dreams
Crisp icy nights it all starts to harden
It's never quite as easy as it seems
You know, never quite as easy as it seems

Bud in the bag is worth two on the bush
But what is already cut cannot be found
In the end when shove comes to push
Might wish you'd never put it in the ground

Eyes were bigger than your garden
Garden bigger than your dreams
Crisp icy nights it all starts to harden
It's never quite as easy as it seems
You know, never quite as easy as it seems

Mandala moonbeams fall on emerald hills
The heat is taking a breather tonight
Ghostly steam rises from the dark still chill
Dancing in the slanted light
Dancing in the slanted light
Dancing in the slanted light

Graphite

Hollywood's gone awful green these days
To listen to all the stars
They sure are busy recycling scripts
While blowing up all those cars

If they ever figured out alchemy's trick
My, how the price of lead would rise
They'd be yanking out ancient plumbing
Scraping graphite from the dots of I's

Might say I'm too cynical
Even claim that it's inimical
Buddha laughs at the rabbinical
Hard to keep my thoughts pure
When no one is really sure
If any of this matters
And if so, to whom

They say that I should abide the law
Not sure I get the point
Of laws that have me waylaid by bandits
And stuck in jail for a joint

We're supposed to all feel terrorized
Let them rifle through our rights
What really causes me insecurity
Is getting groped to catch a flight

And it's the greatest emergency
If the bankers don't get paid
The sky will tumble upon us all
If their bonuses are delayed

Talk about conspiracies
And they'll label you confused
Everyone's got a conspiracy theory
The official story
Masquerading as news
Only question is whose
Crazy theory you choose

Might say I'm too cynical
Even claim that it's inimical
Buddha laughs at the rabbinical
Hard to keep my thoughts pure
When no one is really sure
If any of this matters
And if so, to whom

Does any of this matter
And if so, to whom?
If so, to whom?

Good Friday Experiment

Music by John Kadlecik
First performed by JKB 4-18-14

Castaway summons
Siren calls you on
Promising to explain
When all of this is done
Find it in the mind
Or among the coral reefs
Drift in the aquatic deep
To dream or perchance
Eternally sleep

Meet you in the Chapel
We'll see how deep it goes
Toss the golden apple
Between the wooden rows

The serpent bids you bite
Just a slice of forbidden fruit
Sample some shamanic sight
Before you don your preacher's suit

What is this fire in our eyes
This crazy little thing called god?
Can it ever be quantified
Sized up and demystified?

Let's try an experiment
Can we scan the mystic
Make the soul self-evident
By the light of sight fantastic?

Come ye faithful seekers
This little pill will be your guide
Oh, we'll study divinity
Check out the view inside

What visions will reveal
What wonders will spill
From the ethereal sea?
Let us don our white coats
Complete the quest of alchemy

What is this fire in our eyes
This crazy little thing called god?
Can it ever be quantified
Sized up and demystified?

Let us come together
Pray in Science's name
Learn what kind of faith we find
Taking communion of a different kind

They could not put the genie
Back into the lamp
Could not shut Pandora's box
With their secret stamp
To touch the depths
It is a dangerous thing
Dancing with death
As the siren sweetly sings

Yippie!
An ode to Abbie Hoffman

Air thick with talk of sex peace and race
Paradigms shifting all over the place
Boat rocking from alienation and rage
A paradoxical patriot leapt to the stage

Abbie and his band of merry yanksters
On a mission to mock imperialist gangsters
They were Marxists of the Groucho school
Guerrilla theater their radical tool

Skeptics called their ideas pie in the sky
So they threw the pie in politician's eyes
Stuffed shirts never seemed to get the joke
Chuck 'em if they can't shake a yoke

Yippie!

Called the great unwashed to Washington
To cast out demons from the Pentagon
Couldn't get the warmongers properly high
But angel heads arrived to give it a try

They tried to defy the law of gravity
Allergic to any kind of authority
Sent stockbrokers chasing phony dollars
Got them hot under their starched collars

They blamed him for a generation's unrest
Tried him for putting freedom to the test
Both america's orphan and his father
Stand-up subversive and professional bother

Yippie!

In Chicago the insubordinate freaks
Collected whacks on either cheek
Daley's big show became a fiasco
Blasted by the Yippie torpedo

Abbie knew courtrooms had three rings
Delighted in jerking the judge's strings
Brought elephant and donkey into the act
Charged with conspiring to get his skull cracked

Abbie took the heat for playing in the snow
But he was really a victim of COINTELPRO
Radical clown from the revolution of fun
Went on the run and left a fatherless son

Yippie!

Ballad of The Lost Hippie

It was a typical hippie tale
He wasn't buying the lying
Or wars they were trying to sell
He wasn't cut out to fail
So he grew his mind and hair
And let everything else go to hell

There was no time for college
Far too many worlds to learn
He wanted the kind of knowledge
That brought a more immediate return

So he followed rock's pied pipers
Questing after ephemeral lyric truths
Chasing sonic bubbles everywhere
Before he ran out of youth

Music carries waves of magic
Making mysteries from the tragic
A blast from the past
Restored by vinyl therapy
Music in the key
Of memory

The path led him to an ashram
A peaceful place that felt like home
In austere devotion to inner calm
He shaved and chromed his dome

Clad in saffron selling flowers
Krishna had what he thought he sought
Mumbled the mantras with all his power
Wiping the mind like guru taught

The hippie found himself in too deep
And lost himself a little too well
Not the faintest recollection could he keep
Only rock and roll could ring a bell

So if they say get a real career
That your jams are of no worth
Tell 'em you want to be a sonic doctor
And spread acoustic elixir across the Earth

Music carries waves of magic
Making mysteries from the tragic
A blast from the past
Restored by vinyl therapy
Music in the key
Of memory

Gilded Cage

Cracked my egg in a gilded cage
Penned in tight, a child of rage
Issued me a list of rules and sins
But I didn't know what a mess I was in

I was raised on a diet of lies
On land seized as battle prize
I was trained in the ways of the hive
How to sniff out honey and stay alive

Turn over your daughters and your sons
To be hired hands and hired guns
Swell their offices and prison yards
With idle inmates and idle guards

Oh, my, how they've grown
With a flip of a whip and a toss of the bone
Breeding and weeding tiny clones
Eyes on the tube and ears glued to the phone

I was met by the military shill
Tricked me into signing over my will
Offered to school me and cover my bill
Courtesy of the blood I was supposed to spill

Born in a mess of debt
Owing on a soul I hadn't sold yet
I was bound to break the ranks
Asking do we need these tanks
Rolling on behalf of banks?

When we asked
How does war make us free?
They said it is you
Who are the enemy

Oh, my, how they've grown
With a flip of a whip and a toss of the bone
Seeding and misleading uniformed drones
Until the planet's in a combat zone

I was filled with dreams of a home
Brand-new car glistening with chrome
Salesman said just sign right here
Worry about the price some other year

I reported to my cubicle right on time
Pushing my paper into the slime
Consoling myself with my 401k
Until I read in the news it had all gone away

What can I say, we're getting screwed
Times it seems there's nothing left to do
But occupy the cage and try
To rattle it to pieces till the day I die

Oh, my, how they've grown
With a flip of a whip and a toss of the bone
Feeding the needing of the impulse prone
Burdening the Earth with payments postponed
Till the bubble pops and we're left all on our own

Axioms of Empire

Come now let us rival Nature
Build on banks between the rivers
We shall wall off every danger
Save our stores from starving strangers

We'll set the price of pleasure
Catch our cut from every acre
Tally all the Earthbound treasures
We only own what we can measure

Add a bigger buffer
Around multiplying structures
Divide them up then conquer
Such are the axioms of Empire
Ever hungrier for power
Seeking new realms to devour
Fending off the final hour
As the axe falls on the Empire

These decrees define the letters
Lines confining willful workers
All will cultivate our cultures
For only we'll have any answers

Ordered echoes yoke the future
Designing minds to be their bearer
Wooden actors pose as rulers
Posted half an inch from disaster

We face foregone foreclosure
Debt embedded in the architecture
Interesting how the market's masters
Whip the tribute machine even faster

Add a bigger buffer
Around multiplying structures
Divide them up then conquer
Such are the axioms of Empire
Ever hungrier for power
Seeking new realms to devour
Fending off the final hour
As the axe falls on the Empire

Past the Last Chance

Victory just isn't in these cards
Dreams and waking don't line up
Eyes to the side, stiff and on guard
Nursing an empty bottomless cup
Glancing up from mirror shards
Wondering how it got to be this hard

It is not the fault of circumstance
Nor of the faith you lent
When you took your chance on chance
Your fortune was already spent
Long before you went and sent
All your hollow chips out to dance

I come from a long line of those
Lucky enough to survive
So I'd better wager my last five
Redemption will arrive
When you're past the last chance
Better know the cards in advance

Some times you ante your liberty
Other times it's your very blood
Don't need no crystal ball to see you'll be
Drowning when the gutters flood
Falling with a sickening thud
If you go to gamble with a heart of mud

Worst hard-luck cases get locked into loss
The shift never ends the pay is inverse
The more you mourn it the more it costs
Whole game's a catch and then it gets worse
When you confuse yourself for an empty purse
Heading back into the past and call it a curse

I come from a long line of those
Lucky enough to survive
So I'd better wager my last five
Redemption will arrive
When you're past the last chance
Better know the cards in advance

The Fool

The Fool was always misunderstood
Always kept his eyes on the sky
Dropping out whenever he could
Just a half step ahead of the FBI

Shouldering a humble hobo stick
Puppy nipping at heedless heels
Fool set off in search of kicks
Not a bit worried about the next meal

Found himself nowhere bound
Using blind intuition to see
Never looking down or around
On a quest for lesser destinies

You might condemn such careless ease
You know innocence is no crime
Call him whatever you please
We all play the Fool sometimes
We all play the Fool sometimes

The Fool journeyed to the East
Without any sort of notion why
Skipped into the belly of the beast
And out the back without batting an eye

Randomly turned on a road to the South
Hoping to find some peace and quiet
Wandered down to the Delta's mouth
Stumbled into a skull-cracking riot

You might condemn such careless ease
You know innocence is no crime
Call him whatever you please
We all play the Fool sometimes
We all play the Fool sometimes

Next he took a ride heading North
To scope out the aurora's blue lights
Heedless of the wolves called forth
To halt his unwitting fugitive flight

Twenty-three states wanted him brought in
For wanton negligent criminal sin
But the trail went cold where he'd just been
The luck of the Fool made compasses spin

You might condemn such careless ease
You know innocence is no crime
Call him whatever you please
We all play the Fool sometimes
We all play the Fool sometimes

Amana Mission

There isn't a thing
She can't do with strings
Oh she's a subtle pun
Ever-so-slightly spun
Dreaming of awakening
Ever-so-slightly spun
Dreaming of awakening

It's a lifelong fling
She's my all-in-one
Reason for everything
And she's on a mission
To bring meaning to being
And she's on a mission
To bring meaning to being

Abracadabra
Mystic action now appears
Magic insight sugar spun
Inciting open notions
Abracadabra
With a witch it is done

Just what Chaos ordered
Hands designed for these gloves
Drawing the abstract and absurd
And when I mention love
She is what I mean by that word
And when I mention love
She is what I mean by that word

She's vision wrapped in skin
Finishing what I begin
Wire-wrapped daze planner
Fool's Gold dead-panner
Yo-yo yang flipping the yin
She's the clutch to my pin
And my partner in sin

Stealin' Roses

Put back that fire before you torch the place
Punch a gift horse square in the face
Caught between a clock and a hard chase
You would cut off your rose to spite your space

I used to see you double down on a pair
With a gleam in your eye and knots in your hair
One hand out and the other in the air
Dreaming your way to a fool's nightmare

The house always has the grifter beat
You knew that when you first claimed your seat
But if the dealer spots you trying to cheat
You'll never get out from under the heat

The bridges you sell and bridges you burn
The lies you tell and the fate you earn
The pain you inspire and the chaos you churn
Every action returns
Every action returns
Every action returns

Stealin' roses from the cart on the street
Right next to the very same spot you eat
Lick the boots right off of their feet
Never heard a sob song sound so sweet

Dazzle the others with your magic tricks
I've seen every one, and I'm getting sick
Of watching your candle burn without a wick
Turning the other cheek so both pockets can be picked

The bridges you sell and bridges you burn
The ties you compel and the abuse of concern
You know well the truth you'll someday discern
Every action returns
Every action returns
Every action returns

Some would rather give than make you a thief
Digging deep to spare the benefit of belief
Some would rather spare us all the grief
Run you off with pitchforks just to get some relief

Overdrawn your balance at the bank of goodwill
Foreman's had enough of your plundering the till
Just about everybody has had their fill
Of swallowing your sugar-coated poison pills

Of course you'll be sorry when it's all come apart
The movie's end was clear from the start
Never really was all that smart
Mistaking meekness for weakness
And craftiness for art

Mason Jar
With John Kadlecik

Alpine silver star and angel of abyss
Hunting Horus through history's cryptic mist
Authorized by the Secret Chiefs
To buck every trend and bend all belief
Do what thou wilt, shed the sin of guilt
Push the Sword of Song in to the hilt

Look for the Man
With the Left-Handed Star
Hermetically sealed
In a Mason Jar

The Law commands perpetual awe
Dance inside insanity's jaws
There is no sky there is no limit
Each of us is merely a star unlit
Here is the map if you lose your path
Half of Magick is a just matter of math

Look for the Man
With the Left-Handed Star
Hermetically sealed
In a Mason Jar

Open windows at the Dawn of Gold
Thrice-Great Work done in Divinity's mold
Omens scrawled in invisible paint
Signs seen alone by tainted saints
As veils drop from the inner eye
Spells rise from a well which never runs dry

Look for the Man
With the Left-Handed Star
Hermetically sealed
In a Mason Jar

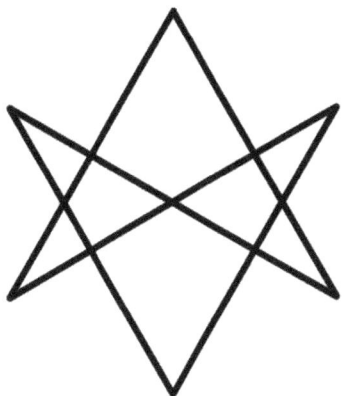

Profit of the Lord

I've come to bring you good news
Go on and sign up, nothing to lose
I'm very sure you haven't heard
The greatest story ever put to words

We'll multiply your bread
By a factor of seven
My upline goes straight to the pyramid head
Oh yeah, the Big Guy in Heaven

I can tell you, hell
It beats selling soap
Way less overhead
Pushing slippery slopes

I work for the Almighty Lord
In a multi-level marketing scheme
Come on and become
Part of the team
You catch a commission
On every soul you bring
When you close the sale
A church bell rings

The Lord needs the money by noon
His credit is fully maxed
And if he doesn't pay up soon
The mob is gonna have him whacked

Running all of creation
You know it ain't cheap
The rising cost of damnation
Enough to make a banker weep

Sure, we're rich in real estate
And fully tax-exempted
But the competition has sex
And even I get tempted

So the economy's bad
You say times are too tough
Getting kicked out of your pad
Hasn't God got it just as rough?

Evolutionists, fornicators
And groovy rock music bands
Devaluing stock indicators
Of our top-selling brand

Our Boss is all-knowing
And infinitely good
You'll break his rules
And He knew you would

His temper's quite hot
Get out of line and you'll burn
The Devil's also got
Commissions to earn

Betty's Attic
With John Kadlecik

Betty never shirked a day of work
She was the picture of the perfect clerk
She never typed off key or lost her smile
Misspelled a memo or misplaced a file

Bosses came and bosses went
She outlasted thirteen Presidents
Betty stayed and oversaw the parade
While over half a century slipped by
Mysteries mastered and history made
As she kept her eyes on the FBI

Secrets of the Universe collecting dust
Up in Betty's attic
Treasures that would test a judge's trust
Up in Betty's attic
A month would not be nearly enough
To tell what's up in Betty's attic
You wouldn't believe even half the stuff
Up in Betty's attic

Betty liked to collect her own evidence
Her paranormal stash was beyond immense
She had artifacts dated centuries hence
Lamps of the djinn and Bigfoot's big toe
Atlantean street signs and statutes that glow
Half a dozen chunks of pure Philosopher's Stone
A fortune in uncut Kryptonite alone

Betty liked to collect her own evidence
Her paranormal stash was beyond immense
She had artifacts dated centuries hence
Lamps of the djinn and Bigfoot's big toe
Atlantean street signs and statutes that glow
Half a dozen chunks of pure Philosopher's Stone
A fortune in uncut Kryptonite alone

Cursed Monkey's Paws
And Loch Ness Jaws
Wizard's wands and vampire's fangs
Vintage vinyl from the final
Concert the Sirens sang
Six preserved pairs of angel wings
And an array of automatic boomerangs

When Betty was found without a breath
Her Attic passed on to Goodwill and dispersed
What they never knew was that it wasn't death
She had simply shifted to another Universe

So if you closely encounter something strange
Sitting on your local thrift store shelf
Search your pockets for forgotten change
Such a strange object could be long-lost loot
Your chance to try a bite of forbidden fruit
From Betty's Attic for yourself

Inkblot Kettlepot

I hail from the far future
Pretending to come from the past
Chaos seeking some sort of order
Where the first always follows last
And symbols are solid cast
When we dwell in dreams
I harbor no doubt
What that was about
Cause I spell out
What frequently seem
Obvious omens
Seen in the stream

I don't like to stew in my steam
Cause temperatures get quite extreme
Flashes like a laser beam
When the whistle finally screams

Oh, the inkblot kettlepot
It's not the pot you knew
Got to be built to get pretty hot
And the lid has a half loose screw
The recipe calls for quite a lot
Bitter words that are partly true
And lots of illusions which are not
But when the boiling is through
What you've hopefully got
Is a clarified vision of you

Under vexing pressure
To prevent venting frustration
Over this twisted situation
Chained to our instruments of liberation
Like a surreal game of tug of peace
Where both sides stand to lose
If the rope is released
Please let's not be confused
We must above all fail to choose
That hasty hesitation
Which kills the moment's momentum

I don't like to stew in my steam
Cause temperatures get quite extreme
Flashes like a laser beam
When the whistle finally screams

Notable Quotables:
ASAOS

"The simplest statements are the most elusive."

"Real art cannot be stopped and it does not need a budget."

"Writers don't give up. Those who give up are no longer writers."

"Words have a way with me."

"As artists, we are only as good as our choices."

"We're writing tomorrow's cliches, today."

"Artists shouldn't cater to the tastes of the audience. Artists are the caterers of taste."

"Everyone can relate to alienation. It may be the only truly Universal emotion."

"There is no reason why all human beings ought not regard their primary function and identity as artistic."

"There are artists with something to say, and artists in search of a statement."

"Poet-tree? Why, that's just the way crazy people talk."

"Poetry does not follow a meter. Poetry produces a meter."

"The verse on the page must match the needs of verse on the stage."

"It's important to write for yourself, but not to yourself."

"Desire is the fire that drives us to strive."

"The thing about music is that it doesn't really sound right unless you can see it."

"Dance is how we answer the question of where to put our hands and feet while music plays."

"My three favorite precious metals: Fool's Gold, Liquid Silver, and Stainless Irony."

"Talent is little more than the predilection to enjoy an activity enough to master it."

"Music ought to have something to do with Muses. But maybe I'm just a Fool."

"No one who truly wants the job of bossing others ought ever be allowed to have it."

"This planet, and indeed this entire solar system, represents the embryonic stage in the life cycle of a star."

"Hippies are discriminated against in subtle ways. For example, parking tickets. We are being penalized for not knowing what time it allegedly 'is'."

"Whenever there are evident shortages of infinite commodities, like energy or information, it's best to suspect a conspiracy."

"Success means there will always be those who come around just to tear you down."

"Any source of abundant energy has creative and destructive potential, which will inevitably be exploited in an equal and opposite reaction."

"One of the biggest lies nearly everyone accepts is that there is an 'energy shortage'. That is absurd. There is no shortage of energy. We are energetic."

"I sold my soul to Gaia for a subscription to the Worldwide Awakening Channel, and I highly recommend the service."

"There is no such thing as a 'free' country. Governments are inherently antithetical to freedom."

"The politics over which one of us is doing it is ruining the is-ness of it all!"

"Bring me your Sacred Chaos for the roasting...."

"The 'truth' is, at best, an estimation."

"Paradox is just Nature's way of saying that your mind isn't open enough."

"We are capable of apprehending far more than we are capable of comprehending."

"Persistence trumps genius every time."

"Aspire to mediocrity, and your success is virtually guaranteed."

"If you approach art as a hobby, you will get amateur results."

"It's not supposed to make linear sense. It's post-rational. We're beyond all that suffocating logic now."

"I like nothing quite so much as having options. I like nothing so little as being out of them."

"If your first impulse is to argue, give it a second and think again."

"Open-mindedness is a trait we tend to value chiefly in other people..."

"The greatest barrier to attaining knowledge is the perverse delusion that we are already sufficiently informed."

"Whenever someone starts jabbering about 'facts', I prepare to hear some unsupported opinion."

"The purpose of conflict is to resolve it. The purpose of pain is to heal it. The purpose of death is honor life."

"We may be mightier than the mountain, but we are no match for the microbe."

"High mojo in the hole..."

"It's half past time to make it happen."

"I am the set of All, I am the set of All I am, the set of All, I am."

"Magic isn't exactly an exact science."

"Make a really weird spell out of a lattice of errors and sanctify it to ERIS…"

"I do not consider the existence of magic to be a viable topic of debate, any more than the existence of color or sound. It exists if and only if you perceive it."

"The difference between a mystical experience and a nervous breakdown is mostly attitude…and the philosophical position of your doctor."

"It's time we de-mystify the mystical. It's all very straight-forward and fairly obvious to any clinical psychotic."

"Demon possession has been unnecessarily demonized."

"Always a day late and a doll hair short with the voodoo…"

"Magic is knowing when to push your luck."

"There was an answer but I was too busy writing down what I'd learned of the question to…"

Some gems from her High-ness, Amana Mission:

"The Mission: To Incite Insight!"

"I art. Therefore I am."

"Sleep is for sheep. Artists collapse into comas."

"We are cohesive, if not quite coherent..."

"I don't trust these writers- they're always plotting."

"Even the most basic patterns will appear as pure chaos until you notice the repeating point."

"The answer to all of your pointless questions is the same: mu. You don't know mu? Go grok mu, and then come back to me."

"Lose your innocence, find your inner sense."

"My way is the high way. I am the scenic route."

Afterwords:
Revised Edition

Everyone's a critic, as the saying goes, and like so many clichés, the phrase sticks because it is an expression of self-evident verity. Evaluating the environment seems a prime occupation of the modern mind; our communications are constantly charged with opinion, estimation, and compulsive judgments about transpiring experiences.

Writing and music are two arts which are particularly sensitive to this dynamic. Audiences, ultimately, decide which artists are considered worth their time and loyalty. Lacking the support of fans, horizons grow dim.

All artistic presentations imply critical evaluations, welcome or otherwise, voiced or unvoiced, which translate into the tone and tenor greeting future expressions. Unforgiving reactions can stifle access to the means of production, and send aspirants back to the day job, or consign over-the-hill veterans to nostalgia status.

Strong material produces strong opinions. If works of art don't inflame a certain amount of outrage and contempt, it is most likely because the artists didn't run with those risky chances required to pursue that most elusive of creative goals: the undefinable phenomenon. The cutting edge often draws blood.

As an avid fan of both literature and live music, I'm acutely conscious of this process. Most of my personal friendships are based on common tastes in authors and musicians, at least enough for a fluid discussions about books and bands to ensue. These conversations become the backdrop for deeper exchanges, where ideas and values are shared and compared, new artists discovered, and quality time logged.

Such relationships employ art as both context and pretext for a human connection that spans a much broader range of subjects. It's what we do when the show ends, to cap the evening, to immerse ourselves in kindred perspectives and have something to shoot the breeze over.

Often enough, there is a difference of aesthetic opinion, and that is perhaps the most instructive of all. We all bring different tastes to the table, which is why the buffet must serve variety.

Audiences assign value to art, consciously or otherwise, according to an intricate and emotionally driven formula, weighing qualities such as familiarity against originality; virtuosity versus simplicity; scope opposed to immediacy. A critique maps art along coordinates of abstraction, framed in the context of similar works.

Each individual prizes different virtues, and there is no accounting for all tastes. Audiences desire something old, something new, something borrowed, something true, in oscillating proportions, defined by, and defining, whoever we happen to be at any given moment.

If any two individuals were to utterly agree on every single point of taste and ideology, I'd venture to suggest that at least one of them is failing to engage in independent thought. Unique as snowflakes, each human mind produces a unique estimation of reality, viewed from an exclusive angle.

There is pretext, and subtext, in all our thought and action. There is what we think we are doing, and what we are actually doing, and often it is the context which makes all the difference.

Originally, this collection was a spectacle of this principle. The pretext was a prank on my songwriting partner, a ritual presentation of lyrics in order to fulfill a joke I had once made to him. The subtext was subtler.

The context is a story for a different time, but suffice it to say that in the rush to publish, things got a bit out of hand, which is why we've issued this revised edition, radically altered and reformulated.

John Kadlecik had first contacted me about *Desert Trance*. This was a song lyric I had submitted two years earlier, via channels, to his bandmate Bob Weir of Grateful Dead fame. John wanted to make a song from the psychedelic vision of a mythical Möbius band, completing the circuit. I thought that sounded mighty fine.

The submission had been handed on to John during a songwriting session for their band Furthur, and I was elated to contribute to the cause. It was an honor to be working with a musician of Kadlecik's caliber. With all due electricity, I began to furiously generate more material for his consideration, a rapidly appearing veritable mountain of verse.

After a while, the piles became unmanageable, as draft versions became obsolete. The online format lacked the texture and portability necessary for serious absorption. As a touring musician, John spends a lot of downtime in transit, and a handy paperback seemed more user-friendly.

Ignoring a host of tremendous pressing mundane concerns, we rapidly assembled the existing material to be printed in time for New Year's Eve, the auspicious moment when we would next see him perform with Furthur.

We entitled it, satirically, *What Does John Want?* (following Tim Leary's *What Does WoMan Want?*) and presented the wrapped package as part of a highly theatrical backstage scene. I carefully chose the optimal moment to drop the punchline.

It was a joke, at the time. Poking fun at frustration is the coping method of champions. Like most jokes, the humor is in the truth of it. The simplest statements are often the most elusive.

Since then, there has been another volume of lyrics, entitled *Rhapsody in Retrograde*, in which the direction of this strange endeavor took a dramatic turn. Instead of catering to some notion of what styles, tones, and subjects John might respond to, I began to find my own voice. That's when it started to flow.

The result was revolutionary. After a long drought, *Rhapsody* immediately accomplished the mission, nailing the target which the first edition of this collection had missed. John began immediately whipping up a storm of new songs.

And the rain did fall.

This version of *Gyroscape*, has, like the author, been through many changes. All of this revisiting of my early efforts, naturally, made me deeply consider the nature of revision, growth, and imperfect processes which aspire toward perfection, which is why I am taking this opportunity to share what I have learned.

If I am to be nothing else, I consider myself to be a model fan. I hope others will follow this example, and become engaged deeply with that which inspires passion and stirs compassion. We all must participate for it to be truly great.

Fanatical indeed, I have devoted my efforts under a set of priorities that can only make sense in terms of madness or a spiritual commitment. People will pull off miracles for that which inspires faith. I *believe* in music. I believe in songs which back the soundtrack of the movie we're all acting in.

I hold music, honestly, as a *religious* principle, because it can be a vehicle for great shifts of emotional tone and consciousness, because live shows provide a pretext for much-needed human community, and, most importantly, because this style of music is an integral part of what has made my own trip a vastly more rewarding journey. Like love, music has made living worth the trouble.

I can take jam music pretty seriously, for someone who couldn't play his way out of a jelly jar, and I don't consider it a spectator sport. I like to get involved. *Really* involved. Playing instruments in public isn't my thing, though, and I only sing well in the shower, where my renditions always make a splash.

On the dance floor, pitching in is simple enough. There, my role is to merely to move in the groove, and it is only my own enjoyment on the line, assuming I step on no toes and throw no unintended elbows. No one but me notices if I hit myself on the nose. Usually.

As a lyricist, though, I must hold myself responsible for the quality of my phrasing. The song must not merely make a statement, it must serve as a fluid element in a harmonious unity, pleasing both the ears and souls of the audience who came in good faith seeking musical glory.

As an active member of these audiences, excellence is the bottom line. The triumphant substance of quality, that mysterious "x-factor," fills the air with the thrill of manifest human potential, crystallizing dreams and expanding horizons. Song proposals must not only match the mindset of collaborators, but the needs of a stage performance where every amplified sound counts.

Transformation is often painful, as we outgrow old selves and bid farewell to cherished follies. The courage it takes to listen to the critic within, to transcend, to evolve, to drive ever higher toward limitless skies has given humanity countless treasures and boundless challenges. I wish this for myself, for you, and for us all, as we collectively pursue the alchemical refinement of Self known as the Great Work.

In the interest of brevity, the precise concise theme driving this note of conclusion, I will only say that I am grateful to you, whoever you are, for being a part of it all. Without you, these are merely words in the wind, and my Fool's gold worthless.

-ASAOS Hx3 W.A.S.T.E.